Collaborating fc
―――――――――――
EDITED BY PEGGY HOLMAN AND TOM DEVANE

The Conference Model

Emily M. Axelrod
and Richard H. Axelrod

BK
BERRETT
KOEHLER
COMMUNICATIONS

Copyright © 1999 by The Axelrod Group

All rights reserved. No part of this publication may be reproduced, distributed, or transmitted in any form or by any means, including photocopying, recording, or other electronic or mechanical method, without the prior written permission of the publisher, except in the case of brief quotations embodied in critical reviews. For permissions requests, write to the publisher, addressed "Attention: Permissions Coordinator," at the address below:

Berrett-Koehler Communications, Inc.
450 Sansome Street, Suite 1200
San Francisco, CA 94111-3320

ORDERING INFORMATION

Please send orders to Berrett-Koehler Communications, P.O. Box 565, Williston, VT 05495. Or place your order by calling 800-929-2929, faxing 802-864-7626, or visiting www.bkconnection.com.
Special discounts are available on quantity purchases. For details, call 800-929-2929. See the back of this booklet for more information and an order form.

Printed in the United States of America
on acid-free and recycled paper.

CONTENTS

Introduction   1
   Voices That Count: Realizing the Potential of Change
   Peggy Holman and Tom Devane

The Conference Model®   7
   The Conference Model: An Overview   8
   What Does It Take to Start?   14
   Roles, Responsibilities, and Relationships   19
   Impact on Power and Authority   20
   Conditions for Success   21
   Theoretical Basis   23
   Advice for Maintaining Benefits   24
   Final Comments   24

Notes   26

Resources   27
   Where to Go for More Information

Questions for Thinking Aloud   31

The Authors   35

INTRODUCTION

Voices That Count: Realizing the Potential of Change

Peggy Holman and Tom Devane

As seen through the lens of history, change is inevitable. Just look at any history book. Everything from fashions to attitudes has changed dramatically through the years. Change reflects underlying shifts in values and expectations of the times. Gutenberg's invention of the movable type printing press in the fifteenth century, for example, bolstered the developing humanism of the Renaissance. The new technology complemented the emerging emphasis on individual expression that brought new developments in music, art, and literature. Economic and political shifts paralleled the changing tastes in the arts, creating a prosperous and innovative age—a stark contrast to the preceding Middle Ages.

On the surface, technology enables greater freedom and prosperity. Yet this century has overwhelmed us with new technologies: automobiles, airplanes, radios, televisions, telephones, computers, the Internet. What distinguishes change today is the turbulence created by the breathtaking pace required to assimilate its effects.

In terms of social change, one trend is clear: People are demanding a greater voice in running their own lives. Demonstrated by the American Revolution and affirmed more recently in the fall of the Berlin Wall, the riots in Tiananmen Square, the social unrest in Indonesia, and the redistribution of power in South Africa, this dramatic shift in values and expectations creates enormous potential for positive change today.

2 THE CONFERENCE MODEL

So, why does change have such a bad reputation?

One reason is that change introduces uncertainty. While change holds the possibility of good things happening, 80 percent of us see only its negative aspects.[1] And even when people acknowledge their current situation is far from perfect, given the choice between the devil they know or the devil they don't, most opt for the former. The remedy we are learning is to involve people in creating a picture of a better future. Most of us are drawn toward the excitement and possibility of change and move past our fear of the unknown.

Another reason we are wary of change is that it can create winners and losers. Clearly the British were not happy campers at the end of the American Revolution. In corporations, similar battle lines are often drawn between those with something to lose and those with something to gain. The real challenge is to view the change *systemically* and ask what's best for both parties in the post-change environment.

Finally, many people have real data that change is bad for them. These change survivors know that "flavor of the month" change initiatives generally fall disappointingly short. In our organizations and communities, many people have experienced the results of botched attempts at transformational change. Like the cat that jumps on a hot stove only once, it's simple human nature to avoid situations that cause pain. And let's face it, enough change efforts have failed to create plenty of cynicism over the past ten years. For these people, something had better "smell" completely different if they're going to allow themselves to care.

Ironically, as demands for greater involvement in our organizations increased, leaders of many well-publicized, large-scale change efforts moved the other way and totally ignored people. They chose instead to focus on more visible and seemingly easier-to-manage components such as information technology, strategic architectures, and business processes. Indeed, "Downsize" was a ubiquitous battle cry of the nineties. According to a 1996 *New York Times* poll, "Nearly three-quarters of all households have had a close encounter with layoffs since 1980. In one-third of all households, a family member has lost a job, and nearly 40 percent more know a relative, friend, or neighbor who was laid off."[2] The individual impact has been apparent in the increased stress, longer working hours, and reduced sense of job security chronicled in virtually every recent book and article on change.

To paraphrase Winston Churchill, "Never before in the field of human endeavors was so much screwed up by so few for so many." By ignoring the need to involve people in something that affects them, many of today's popular change methods have left a bad taste in the mouths of "change targets" (as one popular methodology calls those affected) for *any* type of change. They have also often left behind less effective organizations with fewer people and lower morale. Consequently, even well-intentioned, well-designed change efforts have a hard time getting off the ground.

If an organization or community's leaders *do* recognize that emerging values and rapidly shifting environmental demands call for directly engaging people in change, they often face another challenge. When the fear of uncertainty, the potential for winners and losers, and the history of failures define change, how can they systematically involve people and have some confidence that it will work? That is where this booklet comes in.

A Way Through

This booklet offers an approach that works because it acknowledges the prevailing attitudes toward change. It offers a fresh view based on the possibility of a more desirable future, experience with the whole system, and activities that signal "something different is happening this time." That difference systematically taps the potential of human beings to make themselves, their organizations, and their communities more adaptive and more effective. This approach is based on solid, proven principles for unleashing people's creativity, knowledge, and spirit toward a common purpose.

How can this be? It does so by filling two huge voids that most large-scale change efforts miss. The first improvement is *intelligently involving people* in changing their workplaces and communities. We have learned that creating a collective sense of purpose, sharing information traditionally known only to a few, valuing what people have to contribute, and inviting them to participate in meaningful ways positively affects outcomes. In other words, informed, engaged people can produce dramatic results.

The second improvement is a *systemic* approach to change. By asking "Who's affected? Who has a stake in this?" we begin to recognize that no change happens in isolation. Making the interdependencies explicit enables shifts based on a common view of the whole. We can each play our part while understanding our contribution to the system. We begin to understand that in a change effort the "one-party-wins-and-one-party-loses" perception need not necessarily be the case. When viewed from a systemic perspective, the lines between "winners" and "losers" become meaningless as everyone participates in cocreating the future for the betterment of all. The advantages are enormous: coordinated actions and closer relationships lead to simpler, more effective solutions.

The growing numbers of success stories are beginning to attract attention. Hundreds of examples around the world of dramatic and sustained increases in organization and community performance now exist.[3] With such great potential, why isn't everyone operating this way? The catch with high-involvement, systemic change is that more people have their say. Until traditional managers are ready to say yes to that, no matter how stunning the achievements of others, these approaches will remain out of reach for most and a competitive advantage for a few.

Our Purpose

This booklet describes an approach that has helped others achieve dramatic, sustainable results in their organization or communities. Our purpose is to provide basic information that you can use to decide whether this approach is right for you. We give you an overview including an illustrative story, answers to frequently asked questions and tips for getting started. We've also given you discussion questions for "thinking aloud" with others and a variety of references to learn more.

There is ample evidence that when high involvement and a system-wide approach are used, the potential for unimagined results is within reach. As Goethe so eloquently reminds us, "Whatever you can do or dream you can, begin it. Boldness has genius, power, and magic in it."

What are you waiting for?

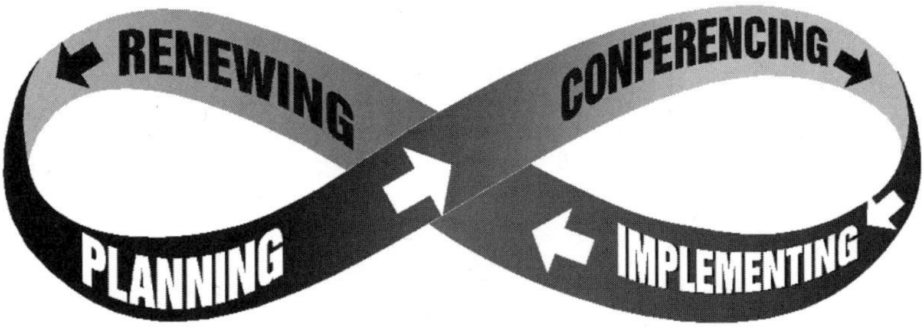
RENEWING
CONFERENCING
PLANNING
IMPLEMENTING

The Conference Model

What we need is to be able to come together with a constantly increasing mind set of wanting to do the right thing, even though we know very well that we don't know how or where to start.

—MALIDOMA PATRICE SOMÉ

For 15 months, Detroit Edison worked to improve its supply-chain process. Despite the hard work and long hours put in by many people from inside and outside the organization, the company had little to show for the effort. Notwithstanding its importance, most people greeted the supply-chain improvement process with disinterested yawns. Detroit Edison had failed to sufficiently engage the organization in the change process.

Today there are 26 active supply-chain improvement projects at Detroit Edison, with potential savings in the millions of dollars. Engagement at all levels of the organization has replaced disinterest.

How did Detroit Edison transform a change process that was on life support into one that is thriving? It used the Conference Model® (CM) to create a flexible response to this critical situation. Not only did it breathe life into the supply-chain improvement process, now other initiatives continue using CM principles to engage the organization in meeting the challenges of deregulation.

Meanwhile, 2,000 miles away, a worried manager had a different problem. "We were like a refugee camp. We worked for the same company but spoke different languages. Shock resulting from a downturn in our industry permeated everyone. We were confused and without organizational homes. Survival meant creating a new way of life," explains Mike Freeman, former director of Hewlett-Packard's Micro Electronics Operation. "The challenges were enormous. We had five different organizations, we were located on one site, and we had to transform ourselves into an integrated manufacturing organization while facing a changing and uncertain market."

Mike and his leadership team instinctively recognized that successfully producing the required changes meant fully engaging the workforce. They used the CM to convert this refugee camp into an efficient, collaborative, customer-focused organization—one that has recorded productivity improvements of 18 percent each year for the last five years. How did they do it? Like Detroit Edison, they transformed the entire organization using the CM.

The Conference Model: An Overview

The Conference Model was the original methodology to engage large numbers of people in systemwide change through a series of integrated conferences and walkthrus. The model consists of four elements:

- a series of integrated conferences,
- the "walkthru" process,
- simple commitments,
- supporting mechanisms.

CM applications include redesigning processes, creating organizational futures, developing new organizational cultures, integrating organizational units/processes, creating self-directed work teams, improving union-management cooperation, and creating organizational alignment with new strategic directions.

The Conferences

What exactly is a conference? A conference is a meeting of the organization's stakeholders and employees at all levels (including important

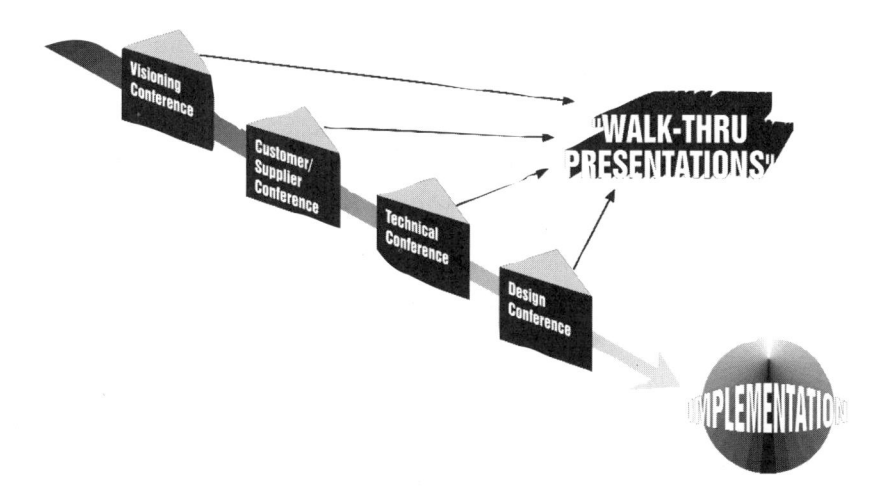

Figure 1. The Conference Model: An Overview

others from outside the organization such as customers, suppliers, and community members). Conferences can range from small groups of 30 or 40 to large groups that number in the hundreds. Detroit Edison's supply-chain process involved more than 900 people (in both conferences and walkthrus) from an organization of 2,500.

Conferences create an open exchange of information, increased understanding of the system under consideration, new agreements and actions, and enhanced relationships among participants.

During a conference, people meet and discuss issues in a variety of formats. Sometimes they are in mixed groups representing all the people at the conference. Other times they meet in stakeholder groups representing a particular point of view. And sometimes they meet as a total community.

Conference participants engage in various activities to increase learning and understanding of the issues under consideration. Conference DNA consists of three elements:

- creating a common visible database as participants post responses to questions on large butcher paper on the wall,

- analyzing the data in table groups and reporting findings to the whole group,
- discussing the data among the whole community.

The databases use a variety of formats to access auditory, visual, and kinesthetic learning styles. For example:

- creating visual maps to identify breakdowns in production processes,
- using ropes that simulate organizational connections to really feel the tugs and pulls in the system,
- burying dysfunctional norms and behaviors,
- creating murals to symbolize a future state.

During a conference, activities build on each other, providing participants a common information base, facilitating analysis and decision making, creating new ways of working together, and stimulating action.

A key Conference Model feature is linking an integrated series of conferences usually spaced four to six weeks apart. Detroit Edison held two three-day conferences, while Hewlett-Packard held five two-day conferences. The number and content of the conferences is determined by the organization's needs. Participants meet in these conferences to understand their present circumstance and identify the future they want to create.

We believe that the complex issues facing organizations today do not lend themselves to instant answers. Few issues can be resolved in just one conference. Crucial to creating high-quality solutions to complex issues is the ability to examine them at increasing levels of depth. A series of integrated conferences provides that mechanism. Multiple conferences also create a critical mass of people supporting the change by involving more and varied participants over time.

The general Conference Model consists of three conferences: a Vision/Customer Conference, a Technical Conference (which also addresses social and cultural issues), and a Design Conference. After the Design Conference, organizations use Implementation Conferences to develop the implementation strategy and to add detail to the template from the Design Conference. A generic Conference Model consists of the following elements:

Figure 2. The Conference Model

The Walkthru

Conferences alone do not create critical mass. You need to connect those who were unable to attend the conferences to the change process. The walkthru process provides that link. Although it was initially seen as less important than the conferences, clients report that the walkthru process is as important as the conferences. Walkthrus are two- to three-hour sessions where conference participants and those who were unable to attend interact and discuss the conference outcomes. The walkthru process is a feedback and feed-forward process. Conference data is fed back to the organization, and walkthru participants feed forward their input into the next conference.

Simple Commitments

The simple-commitment process occurs at the end of each conference. Individuals and groups commit to actions that can be accomplished in the next 30 to 60 days to move the change process forward. Progress on simple commitments is reported at the beginning of each subsequent conference. These public commitments show support and create momentum for the change process. Simple commitments can range from pledging to encourage coworkers to participate in the change process and nurses giving patients hot towels at the day's end to painting lines on a warehouse floor to aid materials flow. These simple commitments move ideas forward while the organization deals with larger systemic issues.

Supporting Mechanisms

Conferences and walkthrus are not enough to sustain a change process against the power of the steady state. The third essential element of the CM is supporting mechanisms: the structures and strategies to support the change effort. They are scaffolds providing support while the change process is vulnerable. These are not permanent structures; rather, they are temporary structures that are dismantled when the change process can stand by itself.

The planning group is an essential supporting mechanism consisting of a multilevel group, including union officials, representing a microcosm of the organization. It is responsible for the overall change strategy. The planning group identifies the goals, guidelines, and boundaries of the change process.

Most planning groups create subcommittees to handle critical tasks. Typically these include the following:

- *The data assist team:* Compiles all conference data and conducts the walkthru process.
- *The logistics team:* Manages on-site arrangements during each conference: set-up, microphones, lighting, seating arrangements, name tags, and supplies such as markers and flip charts.
- *The communications team:* Develops the communication strategy for the process. Since you can never overcommunicate, this group develops multichannel communications, including

newsletters, hot lines, intranets, and lunch-and-learn sessions to share change-process information.
- *The transition team:* Develops the implementation strategy and the implementation conferences and aligns policies and procedures.

Supporting mechanisms also include strategies and structures to deal with negative organization forces that could impact the change process: lack of trust, lack of credibility, prevailing feelings of doubt and cynicism. It can also involve strategies to engage key groups in the change process such as middle managers and/or supervisors. Other supporting mechanisms include union management committees to deal with possible contractual issues.

Costs and Benefits

Is it worth the work, time, and money required to bring large numbers of people together in the CM? The more important question is, What is the cost of not doing it? What is the cost of bringing in expert consulting assistance only to have those plans lay dormant on a leader's bookshelf? What is the cost to an organization when its people believe their voice does not count?

It is interesting that we rarely are asked to cost-justify the methodology. Leaders know that the cost of elegant plans that lie dormant on bookshelves far exceeds the cost of deeply engaging people in the change process. They also understand that the CM produces more than new organizational structures and processes: it produces significant cultural shifts as well. Clients report the following cultural shifts as a result of using the CM:

- *Increased collaboration:* Participants learn skills for collaborating and resolving issues across levels and departments.
- *Increased customer orientation:* Participants learn first-hand about customer wants and needs and how to mobilize the system to respond to these needs.

- *Increased capacity for change:* Occurs as participants use the techniques they learn during the conference to engage others in future changes. A human resources organization that had previously worked with the CM used the process on its own when changing conditions dictated the need to change.

Other important benefits conference participants report include the following:

- *Whole-system solutions* to critical business issues.
- *Accelerated implementation* because high levels of ownership and commitment are created during the process. Instead of the change process's being dependent on a champion, the CM produces hundreds of champions.
- *A deeper understanding of the organization,* its operating environment, and how things actually work.
- *An appreciation of the perspectives of people* from inside and outside the organization. The conference experience creates new levels of collaboration among participants.
- *Increased organizational capacity.* Participants learn immediately transferable processes for group decision making, listening to different perspectives, and identifying common ground in cross-functional and cross-hierarchical groups. They also learn skills to engage the organization in the future.

What Does It Take to Start?

Change always starts with a leader who recognizes the need. Having recognized the need for change, the leader engages others in the process.

Planning

The first step is to convene a cross-functional and cross-hierarchical Planning Group. In union organizations this means including union leadership. The Planning Group engages in the following tasks:

- *Determine the purpose.* What is the intervention's purpose; what do the participants want to be different as a result of their work together?
- *Determine both the case for change and the case for meaning.* What are the logical reasons that this change makes sense and the emotional reasons that this change is important?
- *Assess the current state.* What forces support/hinder success; what strategies strengthen the supporting forces and reduce the hindering forces?
- *Develop goals, guidelines, and boundaries for the change process.*
- *Identify stakeholder groups.* Who has authority, responsibility, influence, and information, and also will be impacted by the change, including those inside and external to the organization?
- *Identify how many people to include in the conferences.* Also decide how many conferences to conduct.
- *Define the selection process and identify people to participate.* We recommend choosing key people—subject-matter experts and leaders—then filling the rest of the conference with volunteers from the previously identified stakeholder groups. We suggest that no more than 20 percent of the conference be made up of people attending by special invitation.
- *Form subcommittees.* The subcommittees handle logistics, communications, and transition planning and form the data assist team.
- *Conduct orientations.* Take your purpose, case for change, case for meaning, goals, and guidelines into the organization. Share information about what you are trying to do and what you want to accomplish, and invite people to join you in the change process.
- *Design the overall change strategy and the conferences within the strategy.* We work with the planning committee to design the

overall change effort, the individual conferences, and the implementation process that follows.

Principles

Also crucial to getting started is developing a deep understanding of the principles at the heart of the Conference Model. Without these principles, an organization risks reducing the CM to a set of mechanical techniques.

Here are the principles:

- *A compelling purpose creates interest.* The task must have depth and purpose. If the task is narrowly constructed without room for new input and ideas, then why bother? Creating a future together is different from providing input to a predetermined course of action. Most organizations concentrate on creating a case for change. Equally important is the case for meaning—involving the heart.
- *Public information and decision making create trust.* Information is valuable only when shared. Thus, all information needed for discussion must be public. This includes all the information developed and decisions made during the change process. Sharing information allows everyone to make informed choices with increased understanding and trust in the whole system.
- *Involve the whole system to understand the whole system.* Effective systems have deep, accurate, and timely communication among the subsystems. When many stakeholders dialogue, they begin to understand each other and the larger system. As they learn how they fit into the larger whole, new possibilities emerge.
- *Create a safe enough environment.* Expressing fear and doubt is key to moving forward. But one organization we worked with called those favoring the change effort *apostles*, while those expressing opposition were called *terrorists*. The terrorist label

caused participants to withhold concerns, which could have led to more robust solutions.

- *Involve the whole person.* We all have a dominant learning style. Some of us are auditory learners, others are visual learners, and still others are kinesthetic learners. When we convene people, we design the process to reach everyone through his or her preferred learning style. When we use only one style, we risk not reaching important contributors.
- *Have a future orientation.* Ron Lippitt's research about groups concluded that when people focus on what they want to create, they become excited and energetic. When they focus on problem solving, they become lethargic. Robert Fritz identified that when people clearly understand both the present state and the future they want to create, structural tension develops, and they move toward that preferred future.
- *Egalitarian spirit builds trust and community.* The answers are everywhere and in all of us. Egalitarian spirit means working together in a way that blurs the privileges associated with roles and titles. It does not mean denying legitimate power or authority, but rather evaluating input on the basis of its worth, not the position of the person offering it.
- *Co-creation builds ownership and commitment.* Ownership is the taking hold of an issue, solution, strategy, or course of action and making it your own. When you own something, you sustain it and see it through to the end. When we make a commitment, we promise to perform, produce, and perpetuate a course of action.

Things to Consider

Before you begin the CM process, there are a number of things to consider, as discussed below.

What are the organization's culture and history? It is crucial to understand the environment in which this change process is going to be placed. To what extent does the CM increase involvement? What is the organization's previous history with change efforts? To what extent have these efforts helped or damaged the organization?

Can management and the consultants form an effective partnership? Each group provides leadership. Management cannot delegate responsibility to lead the effort, and the consultants cannot deny management's knowledge of and expertise in the change process. We believe that effective partnerships require that each group feel 100 percent responsible for the change effort and use its expertise appropriately. The consultants do not have the leadership's organizational knowledge, and the leaders rarely have the consultants' organizational-change expertise.

Do the CM principles fit the organization's aspirations? The previously described principles are a philosophy of work and important building blocks for the change process. Crucial to the effort's success is leadership's understanding and willingness to work with these principles. If an organization does not currently embrace them, is it willing to adopt them?

Is the decision-making process clear and congruent? Our bias is that the process be as open as possible. Boundaries that are too tight do not invite participation. Boundaries that are too loose, e.g., do whatever you want, are not believable and produce distrust. False boundaries are also problematic: we have seen attempts to make the CM process seem participative when in fact it wasn't. Starting the process with a predetermined solution and pretending that people have a choice breeds contempt and resentment. If there is not a choice, then people need to know that. Perhaps participants can then design the implementation process.

Do not start unless you commit to follow-through. The CM engages people profoundly in changing their organization. Enormous energy and hope are created in the direction of the preferred future. If management does not support the process to completion, then pessimism, doubt, and distrust become rampant.

Roles, Responsibilities, and Relationships

Here are the key players in the CM process and the roles and relationships critical to success:

Sponsors

The organization's leaders cannot sit on the sidelines or delegate their responsibilities. Full, visible participation helps leaders understand issues from the different perspectives in the room. In union organizations, union leadership and the organization's leadership jointly lead the effort. Leadership's active participation in the CM produces credibility and trust in the organization. It ensures that leaders' crucial knowledge is available to all, and it ensures implementation because they are part of the process from beginning to end.

Leaders must free up organizational time and resources to support the process and implement the results. Just piling on more tasks to do adds stress to already stressful situations. They must use their power and influence to support the change process and its results.

Facilitators

Facilitation is defined as the process of making something easier. There are several facilitation roles, behaviors, and skills that support a large- or small-group meeting:

- *Boundary Manager:* One key role is maintaining meeting structures—including purpose, boundaries, times, and task. This provides people with a sense that there are things they can count on, and thus proceed with some degree of safety. It makes it easier for people to turn their anxiety into creative energy.
- *Creator of a Safe Enough Environment:* Facilitators cannot guarantee a totally safe environment, but they can stop fights and help most people stay focused on the task. This is done several ways: sticking to the task and time structure, encouraging and

supporting differing voices, asking for opposing views, encouraging people to ask questions and give information rather than judgments, encouraging concrete examples, concentrating on purpose and boundaries, and focusing on common ground.

- *Holder of the Vision:* The facilitator must believe in the possibility of positive outcomes in the midst of chaos, confusion, and conflict. This is not cheerleading but knowing in your gut that people can deal with complexity and will create the order they need. Like any good mentor, the facilitator sees the possibilities in the group before the group members become aware of them.

Participants

Participants must share their knowledge and experience with others. An openness to others' knowledge and experience is also essential. In other words, we ask participants to both influence and be influenceable. People who sit back and observe how it is going to turn out hurt the process, as do those with preconceived ideas who are determined to get their own way. We need people who are willing to come together, build a learning community, and develop actions that no one thought possible prior to attending the conference.

Impact on Power and Authority

The principle of egalitarian spirit profoundly impacts power and authority. Some clients describe it as an exercise in letting go. Others describe it as learning to let go without abdicating. Throughout the CM process, participants work in cross-functional and cross-hierarchical groups. These groups practice communication and discussion skills crucial for the organization of the future. In a very real way the conferences are a practice arena for working in that organization.

The CM does not do away with hierarchy, power, or authority. Rather, participants learn to work with these constructs in very real ways. A directory assistance manager described her experience: "I learned that both managers and operators are real people with thoughts, feelings, and ideas. They are not just roles or titles. There are real human beings here."

Conditions for Success

We have identified the following success criteria when using the CM:

- *Compelling purpose:* As previously discussed, purpose must be linked to a critical business issue and must have meaning. A compelling purpose appeals to both our heads (the case for change) and our hearts (the case for meaning).

- *Leadership:* The organization's leaders must support and live by the CM principles. We recognize that the leaders may not currently behave in a way that is congruent with these principles. What is important is their willingness to move toward them and incorporate them into their management style. One essential leadership behavior is willingness to share insights and information and to be open to the influence of others.

- *Full participation:* Essential to the success of the process is having the right people in the room. This means that all the systems and subsystems are present, all levels are represented, and important others such as customers, suppliers, and in some cases community members participate. Initially many organizations object to including customers and suppliers in the process because they fear they will be airing their dirty laundry in public. In truth, customers and suppliers experience the dirty laundry daily. Our experience is that when you invite customers and suppliers, they become invested in your success and a new level of partnership is achieved. Every client that has invited customers and suppliers to participate in its change process has found it rewarding. The most common statement we hear from clients is that they wished they had included more of them.

- *Patience, planning, and persistence:* The three *P*s are crucial to success. Change is not instantaneous; therefore, patience is essential. The process has emotional highs and lows. Situations rarely are as good as they seem when you are on a high, nor are they as bad as they seem when you hit a low. It takes patience to ride this emotional roller-coaster. It also takes planning. Without planning you do not have a chance of being successful. Careful planning impresses participants and prepares you for the unexpected. Eisenhower said that it is important to develop a detailed plan, and it is just as important to let the plan go in the heat of battle. Persistence is the last *P*. In our fast-paced world we expect instant success. We expect to do it once and get it right. Change does not occur that way. Persistence is a key to success.

Why the Conference Model Works

We believe the CM works for the following reasons:

- *Engagement:* The CM engages the whole system to address systemic issues. The conferences and walkthrus engage the whole organization in identifying and resolving systemic issues. This high level of involvement not only provides unique solutions to long-standing issues, but it also assures implementation.
- *Underlying principles:* The principles discussed in this chapter provide a foundation not just for solving today's issues but for shifting the culture as well. When they are applied, they increase the level of cooperation, collaboration, and trust within the organization.
- *Learning, discovery, and action:* During the process, people learn about the organization, their role, and its relationship to the whole system, as well as how to work with others across

departments and hierarchies. They discover new ways of doing things and identify creative strategies and solutions. They then act through the simple commitment process at the end of each conference or through the strategies and solutions that are developed. This process of learning, discovery, and action creates energy and momentum.

- *Participants who are heard and understood:* The CM works because people experience that they are heard and their ideas count. When it is time to decide strategies and implementation, they can look and say, "I see my idea."

Theoretical Basis

The CM integrates, builds on, and synthesizes various streams of thought, including the following:

Stream of Thought	Source
General systems theory	Ludwig von Bertalanffy
Sociotechnical systems and participatory democracy	Fred Emery and Eric Trist
Future search	Marvin Weisbord and Sandra Janoff
Structural tension	Robert Fritz
Preferred Futuring	Ron Lippitt
Learning theories	David Kolb, Malcolm Knowles, and Howard Gardner
Action research	Chris Argyris
Integration of chaos theory and leadership	Margaret Wheatley
The whole field of group dynamics	J. Richard Hackman, Jack Gibb, Leland P. Bradford, and others
Family systems	Murray Bowen
Ritual	Ivan Imber-Black and Malidoma Patrice Somé

Table 1. Streams of Thought

Advice for Maintaining Benefits

Staying principle-focused is crucial to maintaining the Conference Model benefits. Organizations that incorporate the principles into their daily work life eliminate the distinction between the change effort and doing "real work." It is as simple as asking, "Who else needs to be here?" when meeting to deal with crucial issues. When this happens, the change process becomes embodied in the organization, and the organization increases its capacity to respond to rapidly changing conditions.

Build learning and renewal into your change process. Learn as you go by continuing to ask, "What is working, what is not working?" Ask it of the planning group, conference participants, and those who have not participated in the process. Use this information to make course corrections as you go. Conduct renewal conferences every 6 to 12 months to identify needed changes. Plan for learning and renewal from the beginning, not the end, of the change process.

Final Comments

Common Mistakes

Mistakes we see organizations make in implementing the CM include the following:

- *Being in a hurry:* In today's fast-paced world everyone wants to do things yesterday; everyone wants to rush the planning process and shorten the conferences. They want a gourmet meal and fast food at the same time. It is impossible. We have found that whenever we take shortcuts in the planning process or during the conferences, both the clients and the facilitators pay dearly.
- *Using a cookbook approach:* The process must always be adapted to the client's culture and situation. Using the process without considering the client's unique situation is a recipe for disaster.

- *Letting leadership off the hook:* Success requires that organization leaders be deeply engaged in the CM process. Conference participants need their input, and senior management needs the input of organizational members. Leaders often ask to come to only parts of the conference. Our experience is that this is disruptive because leaders do not have the context. They also send a message that this activity is not really important.

Common Misconceptions

Because the process is so well documented, others infer that it is written in stone. Clients tell us that an essential component of the model is its ability to flex with their unique circumstances.

It is not true that the model can be used only to redesign organizations or processes. The CM and its underlying principles are more than a large-group event—they are a consulting framework and a change strategy.

Notes

[1] Oakley, Ed, and Doug Krug. *Enlightened Leadership.* Denver, Colo.: Stone Tree Publishing, 1991, p. 38.

[2] The *New York Times, The Downsizing of America.* New York: Times Books, 1996.

[3] Holman, Peggy, and Tom Devane, eds. *The Change Handbook: Group Methods for Shaping the Future.* San Francisco: Berrett-Koehler Publishers, 1999. This book contains over twenty such stories of stellar results from high-involvement, systemic change.

RESOURCES

Where to Go for More Information

· ·

Since our focus has been to give you an *introduction* to the Conference Model, we want you to know where to go for more information. Here are books, articles, Web sites, and other sources that can help you develop a more in-depth understanding. In addition, we have provided recommendations of works that have influenced us.

Organization

The Axelrod Group, Inc.
723 Laurel Avenue
Wilmette, IL 60091
(877) 233-8054
(847) 251-7370 (fax)
axelgrp@mcs.com (e-mail)
www.tmn.com/axelrodgroup (Web site)

- *Conference Model Seminar:* A three-day workshop, which provides participants with the nitty-gritty details of how the Conference Model works. Participants experience excerpts from each of the conferences and learn how to facilitate the process.
- *The Essential Skills of Engaging and Convening:* At this five-day workshop, planning teams from different organizations come together to learn from each other while they discover how to engage their organizations in dramatic change. During the week, participants develop a change strategy, plan significant conference(s), and learn to apply the principles of engaging and convening to their unique circumstances.

The Conference Model References

For an extended reading list, call the Axelrod Group or visit its Web site.

Axelrod, Richard H. "Getting Everyone Involved: How One Organization Involved Its Employees, Supervisors, and Managers in Redesigning the Organization." In *The Journal of Applied Behavioral Science* 28, no. 4 (1992): 499–509.

———. "Using the Conference Model for Work Redesign." In *The Journal for Quality and Participation* 16, no. 7 (1993): 58–61.

———. "Why Change Is Hard." In *Perspectives* (Spring 1998): 1–2.

———. "How Four Organizations Saved Time and Increased Commitment." In *Perspectives* (Special Issue).

———. "What Have We Learned? The Conference Model After Four Years." In *The Journal for Quality and Participation* (Special Print Issue).

———. *Terms of Engagement: Changing the Way We Change Organizations.* San Francisco: Berrett-Koehler (forthcoming, 2000).

Videos

The Axelrod Group (producer). *Turn Your Approach to Change Upside Down.* An eight-minute overview of the Conference Model process.

Blue Sky Productions (producer). *Accelerated Work Redesign.* A case history of the Conference Model, 26 minutes. Available from Blue Sky Productions, 800-358-0222.

Newsletter

Perspectives. (For information contact the Axelrod Group.)

Influential Sources

Argyris, C., and D. Schon, *Organizational Learning: A Theory of Action Perspective.* Reading, Mass.: Addison-Wesley, 1978.

Block, Peter. *Stewardship: Choosing Service over Self-Interest.* San Francisco: Berrett-Koehler, 1993.

Bridges, William. *Transitions.* New York: Addison-Wesley, 1980.

Bunker, B., and B. Alban. *Large Group Interventions: Engaging the Whole System for Rapid Change.* San Francisco: Jossey-Bass, 1997.

Bunker, B., and B. Alban, eds. "Special Issue: Large Group Interventions." In *Journal of Applied Behavioral Science,* vol. 28, no. 4 (December 1992).

Collins, James C., and Jerry I. Porras. *Built to Last: Successful Habits of Visionary Companies.* New York: HarperCollins, 1997.

Emery, Fred E., and Eric L. Trist. *Toward a Social Ecology.* New York: Plenum, 1973.

Emery, Merrelyn, ed. *Participative Design for Participative Democracy.* Canberra: Australian National University, Centre for Continuing Education, 1993.

This collection of articles includes an excellent chapter on training search conference managers that addresses the theoretical framework and assumption of the search conference.

Workshop, Search Conference, Whole-Scale Change)

Filipczak, Bob. "Critical Mass: Putting Whole-System Thinking into Practice." In *Training* (September 1995). Minneapolis: Lakewood Publications.

Fritz, Robert. *The Path of Least Resistance.* New York: Fawcett Columbine, 1989.

Hackman, J. Richard, and Greg R. Oldham. *Work Redesign,* Reading, Mass.: Addison-Wesley, 1980.

This is part of the Addison-Wesley Organization Development series. This book does an excellent job of defining the central issues for the design of work. It is also the source for the Job Diagnostic Survey.

Knowles, M. *The Modern Practice of Adult Education: From Pedagogy to Andragogy.* New York: Cambridge Book Company, 1980.

Kolb, David. *Experiential Learning.* Englewood Cliffs, N.J.: Prentice-Hall, 1982.

Oshry, Barry. *Seeing Systems: Unlocking the Mysteries of Organizational Life.* San Francisco: Berrett-Koehler, 1995.

Peck, M. Scott. *The Different Drum: Community Making and Peace; A Spiritual Journey Toward Self-Acceptance, True Belonging, and New Hope for the World.* New York: Touchstone, 1987.

Turkel, Studs. *Working: People Talk About What They Do All Day and How They Feel About What They Do.* New York: New Press, 1997.

von Bertalanffy, L. *General Systems Theory.* New York: George Braziller, 1969.

Weisbord, Marvin R. *Productive Workplaces: Organizing and Managing for Dignity, Meaning, and Community.* San Francisco: Jossey-Bass, 1987. Presents a conceptual and historical framework for organizational change and work design.

Weisbord, Marvin, and Sandra Janoff. *Future Search.* San Francisco: Berrett-Koehler, 1995.

Wheatley, Margaret J. *Leadership and the New Science: Learning About Organization from an Orderly Universe.* San Francisco: Berrett-Koehler, 1992.

Wheatley, Margaret J., and Myron Kellner-Rogers. *A Simpler Way.* San Francisco: Berrett-Koehler, 1996.

Questions for Thinking Aloud

To gain additional value from this booklet, consider discussing it with others. Here are some questions you might find useful as you explore the Conference Model and its application to your situation.

1. In the Conference Model, we emphasize that a compelling purpose appeals to both our heads (the case for change) and our hearts (the case for meaning). Uncover your case for change and case for meaning by exploring such questions as
   - What is your current story?
   - What is the story you want to create?
   - *What will be different as a result of our work together?*
   - What is included and what is excluded?
   - What choices need to be made?
   - What is your purpose?

2. Involving the whole system to understand the whole system is a core principle of the Conference Model.
   - For your organization or community, what is the whole that needs understanding?
   - What connections need to occur between people and between concepts?
   - To reflect the whole system, who needs to be in the room? (Who has authority, information, influence responsibility? Who will be affected?)

3. Successful use of the Conference Model means people need to work together as equals. As a result, the privileges associated with roles and titles blur, and an egalitarian spirit emerges. Think of a time when you've experienced an egalitarian spirit operating. What did you notice about its impact? Why do you think that is?
   - How can you create an egalitarian spirit in your organization or community?
   - What would be different if that were the way everyone worked?

4. Co-creation builds ownership and commitment. When you have been a part of creating something, how did your involvement affect your attitude? How did it affect your participation in making it happen?
   - What is the prevailing attitude toward co-creation in your organization or community?
   - What would it take to make it more likely?
   - How do you see the Conference Model supporting co-creation?

5. We have learned that being able to express fear and doubt is key to moving forward. What happens today when people speak their truth in your organization or community? What would it take to ensure safety as the norm?

6. The Conference Model's walkthru connects those who were unable to attend a conference with the overall change process. In your organization or community today, how are those who are not there informed about the results of important events? What changes in your organization might occur if an effort were made to inform and involve everyone, not just those who participate in an important gathering? How might you help people be more involved in important events and information?

7. Sustaining mechanisms such as planning groups, union-management committees, and communication teams are another key design element of the Conference Model. Think of a successful change effort that you've been a part of. What kinds of sustaining mechanisms were used? What difference did they make? What mechanisms might your organization or community need?

8. If you think the Conference Model is appropriate for your organization or community, what are your next steps?

The Authors

Realizing that in today's world it is no longer acceptable for the few to meet behind closed doors and design for the many, **Emily M. and Richard H. Axelrod** became pioneers in using large groups to effect organizational change. Emily and Richard have a combined 45 years of consulting and teaching experience with educational institutions, Fortune 500 companies, health-care organizations, and government and nonprofit organizations. Emily has a master's in education from the University of North Carolina and a master's in social work from Loyola University. Richard has a master's in business administration from the University of Chicago. This combination of business, education, and family systems gives the Conference Model its unique flavor. The Axelrods believe deeply in creating organizations where equity, fairness, and dignity are present for everyone.

Series Editors

Peggy Holman is a writer and consultant who helps organizations achieve cultural transformation. High involvement and a whole-systems perspective characterize her work. Her clients include AT&T Wireless Services, Weyerhaeuser Company, St. Joseph's Medical Center, and the U.S. Department of Labor. Peggy can be reached at (425) 746-6274 or pholman@msn.com.

Tom Devane is an internationally known consultant and speaker specializing in transformation. He helps companies plan and implement transformations that utilize highly participative methods to achieve sustainable change. His clients include Microsoft, Hewlett-Packard, AT&T, Johnson & Johnson, and the Republic of South Africa. Tom can be reached at (303) 898-6172 or tdevane@iex.net.

The Change Handbook
Group Methods for Shaping the Future

Edited by Peggy Holman and Tom Devane

The Change Handbook presents eighteen proven, highly successful change methods that enable organizations and communities of all shapes and sizes to engage and focus the energy and commitment of all their members These diverse participative change approaches, described in detail by their creators and expert practitioners, illustrate how organizations and communities today can achieve and sustain extraordinary results and foster a capacity to handle the inevitable turbulence along the way. By first systematically involving all organizational stakeholders in the change process, and then planning and implementing change simultaneously—in real time—these methods uniquely enable all members to become change agents, active participants in determining their organization's direction and future.

Marvin Weisbord, Merrelyn Emery, Masaaki Imai, Kathie Dannemiller, Harrison Owen, and many other leading thinkers and practitioners of organizational change show how to harness the vision, energy, and enthusiasm of the entire organization—from employees at all levels to key stakeholders to entire communities. In *The Change Handbook* they provide practical answers to frequently asked questions to that you can choose the methods that will work best in your participative change efforts.

> "In a world where change is the norm, where the effectiveness of organizations is a competitive advantage, and where we have more change methodologies available than most people could absorb in a lifetime, this book has identified how to match the best approach to the situation. While providing structured guidelines for organizational improvement, the authors acknowledge and celebrate the power of creativity and engaged people to provide the energy needed for successful change."
>
> —Susan Mersereau, *Vice President,*
> *Organizational Effectiveness, Weyerhaeuser Company*

Paperback original, approx. 450 pages, ISBN 1-57675-058-2
Item no. 50582-605   U.S. $49.95
To order call 800-929-2929 or visit www.bkconnection.com

Collaborating for Change
Peggy Holman and Tom Devane, Editors

The Collaborating for Change booklet series offers concise, comprehensive overviews of 14 leading change strategies in a convenient, inexpensive format. Adapted from chapters in *The Change Handbook*, each booklet is written by the originator of the change strategy or an expert practitioner, and includes

- An example of the strategy in action
- Tips for getting started
- An outline of roles, responsibilities, and relationships
- Conditions for success
- Keys to sustaining results
- Thought-provoking questions for discussion

If you're deciding on a change strategy for your organization and you need a short, focused treatment of several alternatives to distribute to your colleagues, or you've decided on a change strategy and want to disseminate information about it to get everyone on board, the Collaborating for Change booklets are the ideal choice.

◆ SEARCH CONFERENCE
Merrelyn Emery and Tom Devane
Uses open systems principles in strategic planning, thereby creating a well-articulated, achievable future with identifiable goals, a timetable, and action plans for realizing that future.

◆ FUTURE SEARCH
Marvin R. Weisbord and Sandra Janoff
Helps members of an organization or community discover common ground and create self-managed plans to move toward their desired future.

◆ THE CONFERENCE MODEL
Emily M. Axelrod and Richard H. Axelrod
Engages the critical mass needed for success in redesigning organizations and processes, co-creating a vision of the future, improving customer and supplier relationships, or achieving strategic alignment.

◆ THE WHOLE SYSTEMS APPROACH
Cindy Adams and W. A. (Bill) Adams
Creates a world of work where people and organizations thrive and produce outrageous individual and organizational results.

◆ PREFERRED FUTURING
Lawrence L. Lippitt
Mobilizes everyone involved in a human system to envision the future they want and then develop strategies to get there.

- **THE STRATEGIC FORUM**

Chris Soderquist

Answers "Can our strategy achieve our objectives?" by building shared understanding (a mental map) of how the organization or community really works.

- **PARTICIPATIVE DESIGN WORKSHOP**

Merrelyn Emery and Tom Devane

Enables an organization to function in an interrelated structure of self-managing work groups.

- **GEMBA KAIZEN**

Masaaki Imai and Brian Heymans

Builds a culture able to initiate and sustain change by providing skills to improve process, enabling employees to make daily improvements, installing JIT systems and lean process methods in administrative systems, and improving equipment reliability and product quality.

- **THE ORGANIZATION WORKSHOP**

Barry Oshry and Tom Devane

Develops the knowledge and skills of "system sight" that enable us to create partnerships up, down, and across organizational lines.

- **WHOLE-SCALE CHANGE**

Kathleen D. Dannemiller, Sylvia L. James, and Paul D. Tolchinsky

Helps organizations remain successful through fast, deep, and sustainable total system change by bringing members together as one-brain (all seeing the same things) and one-heart (all committed to achieving the same preferred future).

- **OPEN SPACE TECHNOLOGY**

Harrison Owen (with Anne Stadler)

Enables high levels of group interaction and productivity to provide a basis for enhanced organizational function over time.

- **APPRECIATIVE INQUIRY**

David L. Cooperrider and Diana Whitney

Supports full-voiced appreciative participation in order to tap an organization's positive change core and inspire collaborative action that serves the whole system.

- **THINK LIKE A GENIUS PROCESS**

Todd Siler

Helps individuals and organizations go beyond narrow, compartmentalized thinking; improve communication, teamwork, and collaboration; and achieve breakthrough thinking.

- **REAL TIME STRATEGIC CHANGE**

Robert W. Jacobs and Frank McKeown

Uses large, interactive group meetings to rapidly create an organization's preferred future and then sustain it over time.

Collaborating for Change Order Form
Each booklet comes shrinkwrapped in packets of 6

Order in Quantity and Save!
1–4 packets: $45 per packet • 5–9 packets: $40.50 per packet
10–49 packets: $38.25 per packet • 50–99 packets: $36 per packet

# of Packets		Item #	Price
_____	Search Conference	6058X-605	_____
_____	Future Search	60598-605	_____
_____	The Strategic Forum	60601-605	_____
_____	Participative Design Workshop	6061X-605	_____
_____	Gemba Kaizen	60628-605	_____
_____	The Whole Systems Approach	60636-605	_____
_____	Preferred Futuring	60644-605	_____
_____	The Organization Workshop	60652-605	_____
_____	Whole-Scale Change	60660-605	_____
_____	Open Space Technology	60679-605	_____
_____	Appreciative Inquiry	60687-605	_____
_____	The Conference Model	60695-605	_____
_____	Think Like a Genius Process	60709-605	_____
_____	Real Time Strategic Change	60717-605	_____

Shipping and Handling _____
($4.50 for the first packet; $1.50 for each additional packet.)

TOTAL (CA residents add sales tax) $_____

Method of Payment
Orders payable in U.S. dollars. Orders outside U.S. and Canada must be prepaid.

❏ Payment enclosed ❏ Visa ❏ MasterCard ❏ American Express

Card no. _____ Expiration date _____

Signature _____

Name _____ Title _____

Organization _____

Address _____

City/State/Zip _____

Phone (in case we have questions about your order) _____

May we notify you about new Berrett-Koehler products and special offers via e-mail?

E-mail _____

Send Orders to Berrett-Koehler Communications, Inc., P.O. Box 565, Williston, VT 05495 • **Fax** (802) 864-7626 • **Phone** (800) 929-2929
• **Web** www.bkconnection.com